TABLE OF CONTENTS

WELCOME TO THE ZOO

Buster Bumblechops, expert Moshling collector, at your service! Whether you find yourself lost in the Wooly Wilderness or in that massive home decorating store Yukea, I'm here to help you find what you need to keep collecting those Moshlings!

I'm so pleased to join you on a new Moshling collecting expedition. We've got a ginormous zoo just waiting to be filled with those adorable, elusive little Moshlings, who aren't usually inclined to come out of hiding on their own. You'll need to coax them out and convince them to be adopted into your zoo!

WELCOME!

Buster Bumblechops

Hello there, friend! Name's Buster Bumblechops. Welcome to Moshi Monsters: Moshling Zoo!

WELCOME TO THE ZOO

Monstro City's shops have every supply you'll need for your adventures in the Wooly Wilderness and the zoo.

WELCOME!

Buster Bumblechops

This is the Map. It's how you get from one part of the world to another. You can visit Monstro City and all the shops...

NEXT

WELCOME!

Buster Bumblechops

This is where you will get safari supplies, food for famished Moshlings, and decorations for the zoo.

NEXT

The shopkeepers are ready to help you stock up on Moshling must-haves.

How do you do that? Well, even my natural charms and spiffy hat aren't enough. You must give them what they love most: disgusting delicacies, special items, and the most stylin' zoo rooms imaginable. And then you must keep them happy and healthy once they're in your zoo! Those Moshlings are not easy to please, but as every Moshling collector knows, they are worth the effort (most of the time). I'm still a little mad at Burnie for singeing my eyebrows off.

I can tell you'll be a top-notch Moshling hunter and zookeeper. And probably a stylish decorator, too. The Moshlings are going to love you. Let's get ready for the adventure!

What Are Moshlings?
Where Do They Live?

If you're a first-time Moshling collector, welcome to our elite group of Moshlingologist! Let's begin at the beginning: Moshlings are the Moshi Monsters' pets. They run wild (and mostly hide) in the various Wooly Wilderness areas. Your job as zookeeper is to get all 52 Moshlings to join your zoo, which is where they'll live after they agree to be adopted. You will also need to find all 52 Moshling eggs, which will hatch in your zoo so you'll have brand-new Moshling babies.

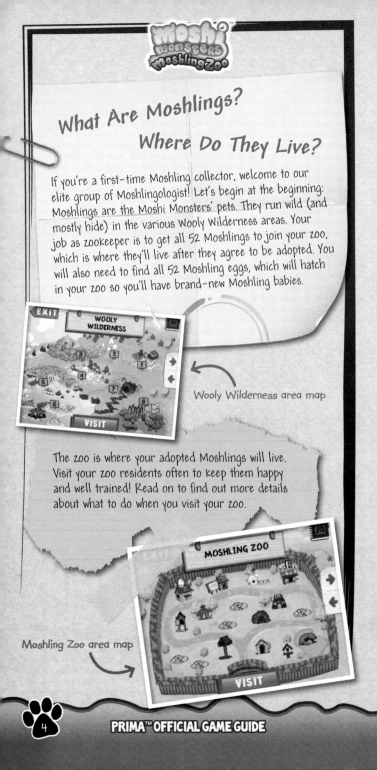

Wooly Wilderness area map

The zoo is where your adopted Moshlings will live. Visit your zoo residents often to keep them happy and well trained! Read on to find out more details about what to do when you visit your zoo.

Moshling Zoo area map

WELCOME TO THE ZOO

Monstro City
area map

The bustling Monstro City is next to the zoo. Monstro City is where you'll buy essential Moshling-finding items with Rox you collect. (More on Rox later.) In Monstro City you'll find safari supplies, Moshling food, and zoo upgrades and decorations. In case you're wondering, I wouldn't recommend eating Moshling food. I tried some toffee toothpaste while I was out in the field once, and I couldn't get my teeth unstuck for a week.

How Do I Find and Adopt Them?

Colonel Catcher, owner of Monstro City's Safari Pro Outfitterz, will be along on your journey to help you find any Moshlings nearby, items to attract them, and lots of encouragement if you get stuck. Of course, I will also be here, and this guide will help you get unstuck from any situation! (Unless you try the toffee toothpaste.)

Colonel Catcher, your
Moshling-catching guru.

The Colonel will give you tips as you explore the Wooly Wilderness areas on how to attract and catch each Moshling. He'll remind you to grab items and tell you how to use them. To get an item, click on it and it's automatically added to your backpack. To use an item, drag it to the Moshling or object you want to give it to. It's easy as eyepie.

Success!

CONGRATULATIONS!

YOU DID A GREAT JOB!
TIKI
WANTS TO BE ADOPTED INTO YOUR ZOO!

CONGRATULATIONS!

YOU FOUND THE EGG FOR
PEPPY
IT WILL GO IN YOUR INCUBATION STATION!

Egg finding means waiting for egg hatching.

Remember to keep a lookout for colorful Moshling eggs, too. Each Moshling species has an adult and baby to collect for the zoo. Moshling eggs hide in the Wooly Wilderness in wacky places—high in trees, low on the ground, and behind shrubbery. They can be hard to find, so keep checking back into each area until they all appear eventually.

Which comes first, the adult Moshling or the egg? As in philosophy, in the Wooly Wilderness, it's hard to say. Sometimes you'll find the grown-up Moshling first, and sometimes you can find the egg before the adult.

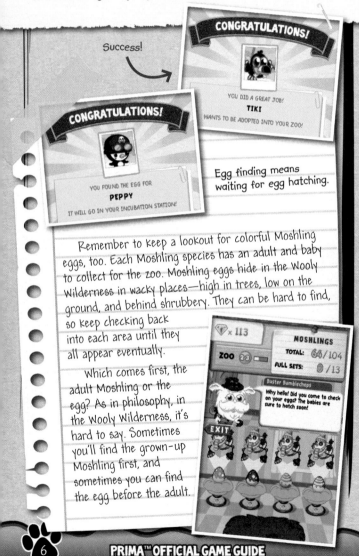

◆ x 113

MOSHLINGS

ZOO 23

TOTAL: 64/104
FULL SETS: 0/13

Buster Bumblechops

Why hello! Did you come to check on your eggs? The babies are sure to hatch soon!

EXIT

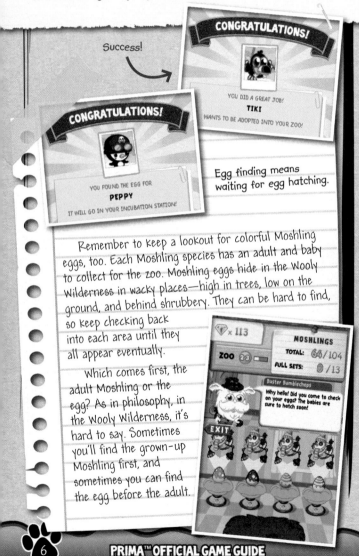

After you find an egg, it automatically goes to your zoo's nursery. You can visit it from time to time, and when it's ready, it will hatch! Baby Moshling! Awwww.

If you're not having any luck with tracking down Moshlings or eggs, exit the area and go back to it again. Moshlings and their eggs will pop up randomly in each area of the Wooly Wilderness.

My most imperative, vital, essential tip (it's important):

Make sure that your zoo is ready for your desired Moshling, or it won't ever show up, no matter how many yummy treats or special items you've bought to tempt it out of hiding. You *must* have the Moshling type's room open and upgraded in your zoo, which means spending some Rox in Bjorn's Konstruction on all the houses and upgrades before you can find all the Moshlings. Home decorating is critical to Moshlings. Hey, they have good taste—after all, they chose you to be their zookeeper!

If you're sure you've got all your zoo's rooms open and upgraded, but are still having trouble tracking down Moshlings, here are some more adoption tips:

- Upgrade and use your Mosh-Ray hint tool on left side of the screen. Depending on which level you have upgraded it to, it can help you find items you need in the environment, or even flush especially shy Moshlings out of hiding! Hit up the Colonel's Safari Pro Outfitterz shop to max out your Mosh-Ray.

- If you find a Moshling but it doesn't want to be adopted, listen to Colonel Catcher's words of wisdom. He knows what he's talking about—after all, catcher is his last name!

- You can buy hints at Paws 'n' Claws for what each Moshling needs to be adopted—or you can keep your Rox and turn to the ever-so-useful Monstropedia section in this guide! It shows you all the hints for every Moshling, so you can save your Rox for more upgrades and items.

- After you've adopted Moshlings, visit your zoo often to spend quality time with your critters. Play games with them—you'll help to train them and earn Rox!

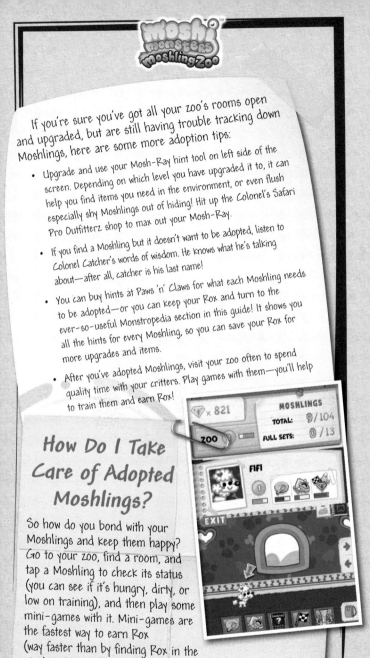

How Do I Take Care of Adopted Moshlings?

So how do you bond with your Moshlings and keep them happy? Go to your zoo, find a room, and tap a Moshling to check its status (you can see if it's hungry, dirty, or low on training), and then play some mini-games with it. Mini-games are the fastest way to earn Rox (way faster than by finding Rox in the Wooly Wilderness, although you should collect those, too).

Turn to the mini-games section of this book for more details on these Rox-earning, happy-making games! After you've trained your Moshlings to higher levels, play the Ulti-Moshling Contest to win trophies!

NOTE

Baby Moshlings can't play the same kinds of games the grown-ups can play, but you can still take care of them and bond with them: Click on a baby Moshling in one of your zoo rooms to play a mellow mini-game. You give the babies what they need, whether it's a bottle or a teddy bear, and get to enjoy their contented little monstrous love. You don't get many Rox for these games, but you do get to max out your own personal cuteness meter.

What Are the Contests and Trophies the Moshlings Can Win?

Moshling mini-game playing means that your Moshling is getting trained better and better to compete in the most prestigious event around: the Ulti-Moshling Contest!

One Moshling at a time competes with other Moshlings (chosen automatically). Your Moshling plays in three games that are very similar to the mini-games you've been practicing. Ulti-Moshling Contest games involve speed, mind, and culinary skills. Although Moshlings can compete hungry and dirty (well, technically, they can...but poor Moshlings!), you must train them in the race and intellect mini-games so they can win here.

The ultimate in the Ulti-Moshling Contest: win a gold trophy for every Moshling! You can admire your trophies on display in the Visitors' Center.

Where Do I Go?

Now that you know what you're doing, here's where you're going!

WOOLY WILDERNESS:
WHERE THE WILD MOSHLINGS ARE

The Wooly Wilderness consists of eight areas:

1. Whoop 'n' Holler Valley: details and map on page 35.
2. Marshmallow Mountains: details and map on page 36.
3. Wobbly Woods: details and map on page 37.
4. Dessert Desert: details and map on page 38.
5. Potion Ocean: details and map on page 39.
6. Taki Taki Islands: details and map on page 40.
7. Kaleidoscope Canyons: details and map on page 41.
8. East Grumble: details and map on page 42.

Go check out each area's map and details in this guide. The map, created by yours truly from hours of time in the field, will show you exactly where to find each Moshling and egg in every area! You will also find tips and strategies for each area, with a super helpful shopping list of items you need to buy for that area's Moshlings.

WELCOME!

Buster Bumblechops

travel out to the Wooly Wilderness on Safari with Colonel Catcher to find Moshlings and convince them to join your zoopalooza...

NEXT

MOSHLING ZOO:
WHERE THE ADOPTED MOSHLINGS ARE

EXIT MOSHLING ZOO

VISIT

The starting zoo...

EXIT MOSHLING ZOO

VISIT

...and the bursting-with-Moshlings zoo!

The zoo consists of 17 areas:

MOSHLING ZOO

EXIT

VISIT

1. Buster's Baby Care

Where eggs go to hatch when they're good and ready.

2. Visitors' Center

Here you can read through the Monstropedia, or admire your trophies.

3. Glormatorium

The Grub Hub, where you can play the Moshling feeding mini-game, and the Rubbadub Pool, where you can play the Moshling bathing mini-game.

4. Raarghly's Starcade

You can play the Quik Wits and Rapid Matches mini-games here.

5. Beasties

Room available at start of game.

6. Birdies

Room available at start of game.

7. Dinos

Room not available at start of game—must purchase upgrade from Bjorn's Konstruction to make room available.

8. Fishies

Room available at start of game.

4. Fluffies

Room available at start of game.

10. Foodies

Room available at start of game.

11. Kitties

Room available at start of game.

12. Ponies

Room available at start of game.

13. Puppies

Room available at start of game.

14. Spookies

Room not available at start of game—must purchase upgrade from Bjorn's Konstruction to make room available.

15. Techies

Room not available at start of game—must purchase upgrade from Bjorn's Konstruction to make room available.

16. Worldies

Room not available at start of game—must purchase upgrade from Bjorn's Konstruction to make room available.

17. Ninjas

Room not available at start of game—must purchase upgrade from Bjorn's Konstruction to make room available.

MONSTRO CITY: WHERE THE WILD MOSHLING HUNTER GOES SHOPPING

Monstro City features seven shops where you can buy everything you need to attract new Moshlings and keep them happy in your zoo. Bet you didn't know this, but I'm not only an expert Moshling hunter, I'm your personal shopping guide, too! To be an expert Moshling hunter, you have to be a great shopper. Read on for a tour of all the items you'll find in each shop, how many Rox you'll need to purchase each item, if you need to purchase an item from the shop, and which Moshlings will most appreciate your purchases!

If my tables say you don't need to buy an item from a shop, that means you can find it in the Wooly Wilderness for free. Items are always in the same area as the Moshlings who want them.

Paws 'n' Claws

Shopkeeper: Gilbert Finnster

Paws 'n' Claws sells hints for how to get every Moshling in each category. This is where you can go when you are stumped for how to find that Moshling who's playing hard to get. However, since you have wisely acquired my book, you can check this guide's Monstropedia section for hints for each Moshling and save your Rox for other goodies!

Item for Sale	Must Buy in Shop?	Price in Rox	Sales Pitch	Who It's For
Fluffies Hints	Yes*	500	Clues that go into your Monstropedia to collect all the Fluffies!	Dipsy, Flumpy, Honey, I.G.G.Y.
Puppies Hints	Yes*	500	Having a ruff time gathering all the Puppies? Buy these hints and solve your problems!	Fifi, McNulty, Scamp, White Fang
Beasties Hints	Yes*	750	Buying this will give you hints for how to capture all of the Beasties!	Burnie, Humphrey, Jeepers, ShiShi
Kitties Hints	Yes*	750	Needing some purrfect hints on how to capture all of the Kitties? Look no further!	Gingersnap, Lady Meowford, Purdy, Waldo
Ponies Hints	Yes*	1,000	It takes more than carrots to adopt these Ponies! Check your Monstropedia after you buy!	Angel, Gigi, Mr. Snoodle, Priscilla
Birdies Hints	Yes*	1,000	Want to know how to nab all the Birdies? Buy these hints for your Monstropedia!	DJ Quack, Peppy, Prof. Purplex, Tiki
Foodies Hints	Yes*	1,250	Your Foodie hint guide. All Foodies, all the time. Check your Monstropedia!	Coolio, Cutie Pie, Hansel, Oddie
Dinos Hints	Yes*	1,250	Purchase this for hints on how to capture the Dinos before they become extinct.	Doris, Gurgle, Pooky, Snookums
Fishies Hints	Yes*	1,500	Need some more clues on hooking Fishies? Buy these hints and your nets will overflow!	Blurp, Cali, Fumble, Stanley

Item for Sale	Must Buy in Shop?	Price in Rox	Sales Pitch	Who It's For
Ninja Hints	Yes*	1,500	Want to know how to waylay all the Ninjas? Buy these hints for your Monstropedia!	Chop Chop, General Fuzuki, Shelby, Sooki-Yaki
Spookies Hints	Yes*	1,500	I have a feeling that if you buy this, clues will appear on how to collect the Spookies!	Big Bad Bill, Ecto, Kissy, Squidge
Worldies Hints	Yes*	1,750	You don't have to travel all over to adopt the Worldies, but if you need hints, buy this!	Cleo, Liberty, Mini Ben, Rocky
Techies Hints	Yes*	1,750	Techies want to be adopted, but they don't make it easy. Buy this if you need some clues.	Gabby, Holga, Nipper, Wurley

TIP

*Or, you can save your Rox and check this guide's Monstropedia section for hints for every Moshling!

Gross-ery Store

Shopkeeper: Snozzle Wobbleson

Find all your Moshling delicacies here. What Moshling could resist such disgustingly delicious treats?

WELCOME TO THE ZOO

Item for Sale	Must Buy in Shop?	Price in Rox	Sales Pitch	Who It's For
Marmalade with Bits	No* *Free at start	10	This super sugary mixture of wild Spoanges and Candiflop fruits will stick to your tummy.	Dipsy in Whoop 'n' Holler Valley
Carroty Cake	Yes	100	Half carrot, two-fourths cake, completely delicious.	Honey in Whoop 'n' Holler Valley
Common Cotton Candy	Yes	50	Beloved by royalty and peasants alike.	Angel in Marshmallow Mountains, Gigi in Kaleidoscope Canyons
Pumpernickle Bread Crumbs	Yes	75	Crumbled off Pumperdime Bread.	Mr. Snoodle in Dessert Desert
Sucker Punch Drink	Yes	25	What kind of sucker? Why don't you take a sip and find out?	Tiki in Potion Ocean
Slop	Yes	50	Tastes disgusting, looks vile, that's Slop alright.	Feed to any Moshling in your zoo
Grande Gateau	Yes	200	Not one, not two, but three layers of yummy gateaux. Eat in moderation.	Feed to any Moshling in your zoo
Carton of Sour Milk	Yes	25	Nutritious, healthy milk left in the sun for a few days.	Feed to any Moshling in your zoo

Item for Sale	Must Buy in Shop?	Price in Rox	Sales Pitch	Who It's For
Quenut Butter Sandwich	Yes	75	Made with real quenuts.	Feed to any Moshling in your zoo
Toffee Nachos	Yes	50	The beginning of many a squabble. Hey, this is na-cho toffee!	Waldo in Marshmallow Mountains
Silly Chili	Yes	35	Little peppers that just can't sit still.	Feed to any Moshling in your zoo
Swirlberry Muffin	Yes	75	Winner of the Tallest Swirl of the Year award.	Feed to any Moshling in your zoo
Slamburger	Yes	50	Like a normal burger, but slammed to perfection.	Feed to any Moshling in your zoo
Slopcorn	Yes	30	The gunkiest movie-snack around.	Feed to any Moshling in your zoo
Crispy Bat Wings	Yes	75	Sonar-fried for extra crunch.	Feed to any Moshling in your zoo
Eyepie	Yes	50	The snack that stares back.	Feed to any Moshling in your zoo
Pepper Popcorn	Yes	50	Sneeze through the latest hit movie.	Feed to any Moshling in your zoo

WELCOME TO THE ZOO

Item for Sale	Must Buy in Shop?	Price in Rox	Sales Pitch	Who It's For
Cup o' Gruel	Yes	50	Have some more.	Feed to any Moshling in your zoo
Sludge Fudge	Yes	50	Eat it fast before it drips off your plate.	Feed to any Moshling in your zoo
Pumpkin Chowder	Yes	50	Best served on Halloween.	Feed to any Moshling in your zoo
Spider Lolly	Yes	50	Eight legs of flavor	Feed to any Moshling in your zoo
Roast Beast	Yes	75	Just like mother used to roast.	Feed to any Moshling in your zoo
Eyescream	Yes	100	Like roarberry cheesecake, but with half the decibels.	Feed to any Moshling in your zoo
Chocolate Coated Broccoli	Yes	50	Worse than it sounds.	Feed to any Moshling in your zoo
Eggplant	Yes	50	A plant with eggs, what were you expecting?	Feed to any Moshling in your zoo
Fango Mandango	Yes	100	The dancing fruit.	Feed to any Moshling in your zoo
Toad Soda	Yes	50	From the makers of Croak-a-Cola. Contains real toad.	Feed to any Moshling in your zoo

Item for Sale	Must Buy in Shop?	Price in Rox	Sales Pitch	Who It's For
Bug Juice	Yes	50	Squeezed on the fly for extra bug!	Feed to any Moshling in your zoo
Fly Trap Salad	Yes	75	It bites back!	Feed to any Moshling in your zoo
Rat Tail Spaghetti	Yes	50	Guaranteed free from mouse tail.	Feed to any Moshling in your zoo

* The marmalade can't be found in the environment, but it's the only item you start out with automatically.

Yukea

Shopkeeper: Moe Yukky

Yukea is a one-stop shop for spiffying up your Moshlings' zoo homes. You wouldn't want your Moshlings to live with poor interior design, would you? Of course not. Turn to Yukea for all your decorating needs.

WELCOME TO THE ZOO

Item for Sale	Must Buy in Shop?	Price in Rox	Sales Pitch	Who It's For
Beasties Decoration	Yes	Level 1 250 / Level 2 250 / Level 3 250	These pieces of rustic flair will make the Beasties' pad even more RAAAW-some!	Burnie, Humphrey, Jeepers, ShiShi
Birdies Decoration	Yes	Level 1 500 / Level 2 500 / Level 3 500	Bling out the Birdies' digs and put the tweet in sweet with these bird cage buys.	DJ Quack, Peppy, Prof. Purplex, Tiki
Dinos Decoration	Yes	Level 1 500 / Level 2 500 / Level 3 500	It's getting all prehistoric up in here with thingies to make the Dinos' place rock.	Doris, Gurgle, Pooky, Snookums
Fishies Decoration	Yes	Level 1 750 / Level 2 750 / Level 3 750	Make a splash in the Fishies' home with these underwater ornaments.	Blurp, Cali, Fumble, Stanley
Fluffies Decoration	Yes	Level 1 750 / Level 2 750 / Level 3 750	This piece of finery will take the Fluffies' paradise to cloud nine.	Dipsy, Flumpy, Honey, I.G.G.Y.
Foodies Decoration	Yes	Level 1 1,000 / Level 2 1,000 / Level 3 1,000	Decorations are like sprinkles. They just make the Foodies' place even more delicious.	Coolio, Cutie Pie, Hansel, Oddie
Kitties Decoration	Yes	Level 1 1,000 / Level 2 1,000 / Level 3 1,000	More cuddly knickknack goodness for the Kitties' romping room.	Gingersnap, Lady Meowford, Purdy, Waldo

Item for Sale	Must Buy in Shop?	Price in Rox	Sales Pitch	Who It's For
Ninjas Decoration	Yes	Level 1 1,250	Even cunning Ninjas' dojos need some beautification from time to time.	Chop Chop, General Fuzuki, Shelby, Sooki-Yaki
		Level 2 1,250		
		Level 3 1,250		
Ponies Decoration	Yes	Level 1 1,250	Ponies like to play, so pretty-ify up their place with something fun!	Angel, Gigi, Mr. Snoodle, Priscilla
		Level 2 1,250		
		Level 3 1,250		
Puppies Decoration	Yes	Level 1 1,500	These treats will make the Puppies' pen a lap of luxury.	Fifi, McNulty, Scamp, White Fang
		Level 2 1,500		
		Level 3 1,500		
Spookies Decoration	Yes	Level 1 1,750	The Spookies' haunted home needs some scary fripperies to make it more monsterific.	Big Bad Bill, Ecto, Kissy, Squidge
		Level 2 1,750		
		Level 3 1,750		
Techies Decoration	Yes	Level 1 1,750	Technical decorations are the nuts and bolts of a good Techie's domicile.	Gabby, Holga, Nipper, Wurley
		Level 2 1,750		
		Level 3 1,750		
Worldies Decoration	Yes	Level 1 2,000	These antiquated bits of finery will make the Worldies' abode even more well traveled.	Cleo, Liberty, Mini Ben, Rocky
		Level 2 2,000		
		Level 3 2,000		

Bjorn's Konstruction

Shopkeeper: Bjorn, of course

Bjorn's sales pitch might be only a few words (okay, so they're all the same words), but don't let that fool you: you need Bjorn and his habitat upgrades. Moshlings can be very persnickety about their homes. You want your zoo habitats to be the biggest and best they can be, so do lots of remodeling and buy every habitat upgrade as soon as you can. You can't attract all the Moshlings without having your habitats upgraded to the max.

Item for Sale	Must Buy in Shop?	Price in Rox	Sales Pitch	Who It's For
Fluffies House Upgrade	Yes	Level 1 250	Ready to build this beautiful Moshling habitat?	Dipsy, Flumpy, Honey, I.G.G.Y.
		Level 2 250		
		Level 3 250		
Puppies House Upgrade	Yes	Level 1 250	Ready to build this beautiful Moshling habitat?	Fifi, McNulty, Scamp, White Fang
		Level 2 250		
		Level 3 250		
Beasties House Upgrade	Yes	Level 1 500	Ready to build this beautiful Moshling habitat?	Burnie, Humphrey, Jeepers, ShiShi
		Level 2 500		
		Level 3 500		

Item for Sale	Must Buy in Shop?	Price in Rox	Sales Pitch	Who It's For
Kitties House Upgrade	Yes	Level 1 500	Ready to build this beautiful Moshling habitat?	Gingersnap, Lady Meowford, Purdy, Waldo
		Level 2 500		
		Level 3 500		
Ponies House Upgrade	Yes	Level 1 500	Ready to build this beautiful Moshling habitat?	Angel, Gigi, Mr. Snoodle, Priscilla
		Level 2 500		
		Level 3 500		
Birdies House Upgrade	Yes	Level 1 750	Ready to build this beautiful Moshling habitat?	DJ Quack, Peppy, Prof. Purplex, Tiki
		Level 2 750		
		Level 3 750		
Foodies House Upgrade	Yes	Level 1 750	Ready to build this beautiful Moshling habitat?	Coolio, Cutie Pie, Hansel, Oddie
		Level 2 750		
		Level 3 750		
Dinos House Upgrade	Yes	Level 1 750	Ready to build this beautiful Moshling habitat?	Doris, Gurgle, Pooky, Snookums
		Level 2 750		
		Level 3 750		
Fishies House Upgrade	Yes	Level 1 1,000	Ready to build this beautiful Moshling habitat?	Blurp, Cali, Fumble, Stanley
		Level 2 1,000		
		Level 3 1,000		

Item for Sale	Must Buy in Shop?	Price in Rox	Sales Pitch	Who It's For
Ninjas House Upgrade	Yes	Level 1 1,000	Ready to build this beautiful Moshling habitat?	Chop Chop, General Fuzuki, Shelby, Sooki-Yaki
		Level 2 1,000		
		Level 3 1,000		
Spookies House Upgrade	Yes	Level 1 1,000	Ready to build this beautiful Moshling habitat?	Big Bad Bill, Ecto, Kissy, Squidge
		Level 2 1,000		
		Level 3 1,000		
Worldies House Upgrade	Yes	Level 1 1,250	Ready to build this beautiful Moshling habitat?	Cleo, Liberty, Mini Ben, Rocky
		Level 2 1,250		
		Level 3 1,250		
Techies House Upgrade	Yes	Level 1 1,250	Ready to build this beautiful Moshling habitat?	Gabby, Holga, Nipper, Wurley
		Level 2 1,250		
		Level 3 1,250		

Bizarre Bazaar

Shopkeeper: Bushy Fandango

You'll be seeing a lot of this shop and its pink-eared shopkeeper because it's got specialty items to attract and appease particularly picky Moshlings. But don't spend all your Rox in one place: remember that many items sold here can be found in the wild area your desired Moshling inhabits, so you don't need to buy everything here (but don't tell Bushy I said that).

Item for Sale	Must Buy in Shop?	Price in Rox	Sales Pitch	Who It's For
Silly Sausages	Yes	25	Don't listen to their knock-knock jokes—they are just terrible.	Burnie in Taki Taki Islands
Deep Fried Oobladoobla	Yes for all	25	It's a doobla inside an oobla, dipped in batter and fried to golden perfection.	Big Bad Bill in Wobbly Woods, Oddie in Dessert Desert
Stuffy Stuffing	Yes	25	Inside a turkey, inside a pillow, is there a bad place to keep this snack?	Feed to any Moshling in your zoo
Runny Custard	Yes	25	Far less fatty than sit-on-the-couchy custard. Perfect for bathing in.	Hansel in Kaleidoscope Canyons
Power Pastry	Yes	25	Ready to pump up your gut.	Purdy in Kaleidoscope Canyons
Toe-mato Soup	Yes	35	Mato Fingers cost extra.	Squidge in Kaleidoscope Canyons
Hot Sweet Tea	Yes	35	It's hot, Sweetie!	Feed to any Moshling in your zoo
Guzzly Gasoline	No for all	35	Not for animal consumption.	Wurley in Dessert Desert, Burnie in Taki Taki Islands

Item for Sale	Must Buy in Shop?	Price in Rox	Sales Pitch	Who It's For
Fairy Cake	Yes	35	Eat it quick before it flutters away!	Feed to any Moshling in your zoo
Starlight Cookies	Yes	35	The biscuits that fell to earth.	Feed to any Moshling in your zoo
Trash Can Surprise	Yes	40	Every bite is a tastebud adventure!	Feed to any Moshling in your zoo
Roarberry Cheesecake	Yes	40	Louder than your average dessert.	Feed to any Moshling in your zoo
Kandy Kane	Yes	40	Twist and turn as you chew this Twistmassy Kandy.	Feed to any Moshling in your zoo
Mississippi Mud Pie	Yes	40	Now with real mud.	Feed to any Moshling in your zoo
Pop Rox	Yes	40	Pop them in your mouth and Rox your tastebuds!	Feed to any Moshling in your zoo
Swirly Sea Oats	No	65	Wild oats sown at sea.	Stanley in Potion Ocean
Sunshine Berries	Yes	80	The brightest fruit around.	Feed to any Moshling in your zoo

Item for Sale	Must Buy in Shop?	Price in Rox	Sales Pitch	Who It's For
Flippity Flops	No	75	Most gymnastic shoes around.	Blurp in Taki Taki Islands
Mosh-Day Planner	No	65	One stop for all your mosh-scheduling.	Blurp in Taki Taki Islands
Toffee Toothpaste	No	50	For filling in those sugar cavities.	Shelby in Potion Ocean
Paint Brush	No	80	Art made with this brush will take your breath away.	Jeepers in Wobbly Woods
Moon Orchid Seed	No	50	The best flowers to attract Rummaging Plotamususes.	Doris in Wobbly Woods
Twangy Banjo Strings	No	75	To be added to a twangy banjo.	Humphrey in Whoop 'n' Holler Valley
Fruity Furniture Polish	No	70	Lemon, Watermelon, Dragonfruit, who knows what this will make your home smell like!	Flumpy in Whoop 'n' Holler Valley
Sparkly Candy Apples	Yes	100	A feast for your eyes and your mouth.	Priscilla in Dessert Desert
Tickly Pickle	Yes	125	Pairs well with a Giggly Gizzard.	I.G.G.Y. in East Grumble

Horrods

Shopkeeper: Mizz Snoots

In addition to getting a gander at Mizz Snoots's lime-green lipstick, here you'll find the perfect little luxuries for your Moshlings. Horrods stocks CDs for your music-loving Moshling (check the Monstropedia section of the guide or in-game to find out what kind of music makes your Moshling get its groove on!). For the more sensitive Moshlings, you can even find extra soft tissues for monstrously tender noses.

Item for Sale	Must Buy in Shop?	Price in Rox	Sales Pitch	Who It's For
Harp CD	No	400	A fine collection of harp music.	Fifi in Whoop 'n' Holler Valley
Calm CD	No	550	A fine collection of calm music.	Snookums in East Grumble
Marimba CD	No	450	A fine collection of marimba music.	Gigi in Kaleidoscope Canyons
Funky CD	No	550	A fine collection of fast funky disco music.	DJ Quack in Taki Taki Islands
Egyptian CD	No	600	A fine collection of Egyptian music.	Stanley in Potion Ocean

Item for Sale	Must Buy in Shop?	Price in Rox	Sales Pitch	Who It's For
Rock CD	No	650	A fine collection of rock music.	Cali in Potion Ocean
Soft CD	No	700	A fine collection of soft music.	Dipsy in Whoop 'n' Holler Valley, Mr. Snoodle in Dessert Desert
Roarex Watch	No	1,200	I promise it isn't a knock-off.	Mini Ben in East Grumble
Pink Ribbon	No	375	When blue ribbon just isn't good enough.	Kissy in Kaleidoscope Canyons
Cower Cape	No	700	Does the cape cause you to cower or your enemies?	Squidge in Kaleidoscope Canyons
Extra Soft Tissues	Yes for all	250	Somewhere between soft tissues and extra extra soft tissues.	ShiShi in Wobbly Woods, Shelby in Potion Ocean, Gurgle in Kaleidoscope Canyons
Cardboard Celebrity	Yes	2,000	The next best thing to an actual celebrity.	Holga in Taki Taki Islands

Safari Pro Outfitterz

Shopkeeper: Colonel Catcher

You can find many of the Colonel's items hiding in the Wooly Wilderness, but you should still visit the Colonel (and not just to admire his impressive mustache). He's got a very special item: the Mosh-Ray upgrade, levels 2 and 3. Upgrading your Mosh-Ray will help you discover any shy Moshlings that are lurking about. (Keep in mind that even with a maxed out Mosh-Ray, you have to have all the houses ready and upgraded before all Moshlings will come out of hiding.)

Item for Sale	Must Buy in Shop?	Price in Rox	Sales Pitch	Who It's For
Mosh-Ray Level 2	Yes	1,500	This Mosh-ray upgrade shows you where Moshlings are hiding.	Any Moshling
Mosh-Ray Level 3	Yes	6,000	This ultimate upgrade will persuade Moshlings to be adopted instantly!	Any Moshling
Super Shovel	Yes	50	Can shovel large rocks—or anything else—in a single scoop.	Any Moshling
Terry's Towel	Yes for all	25	Terry is gonna be mad someone sold his towel.	Scamp in Whoop 'n' Holler Valley, ShiShi in Wobbly Woods, McNulty in East Grumble

moshi monsters moshling Zoo

Item for Sale	Must Buy in Shop?	Price in Rox	Sales Pitch	Who It's For
Needlekins & Thready	Yes for all	25	Quite the dynamic duo.	Gingersnap in Marshmallow Mountains, Cutie-Pie in Dessert Desert
Umbrella Spring	No for all	400	Gives your broken umbrella the lift it's been missing, for a shadow of the glory days.	Ecto in Marshmallow Mountains, Coolio in Dessert Desert
Mr. Moustache Wax	No	25	Not your mother's mustache wax. It's Colonel Catcher's favorite!	Mini Ben in East Grumble
Triple-ZZZ Batteries	No	25	For use on power naps.	Liberty in Taki Taki Islands
Bang-up Bandages	Yes for all	25	Bang-up Bandages for bang up bang-ups!	Fumble in Taki Taki Islands, Sooki-Yaki in East Grumble
Big Ol' Bucket	No	25	Not to be confused with the Little Ol' Dipper.	Cleo in Dessert Desert
Cocoa Hose	No	25	For transportation of pure chocolatey goodness.	Cutie Pie in Dessert Desert
Magical Magnifying Glass	No	25	Magically magnifies glass!	McNulty in East Grumble

Item for Sale	Must Buy in Shop?	Price in Rox	Sales Pitch	Who It's For
Mighty Matches	No	25	Small in size, great in power.	Sooki-Yaki in East Grumble
Trusty Treasure Map	No	25	It's supposed to lead to the Golden City of Moshlantis.	Cleo in Dessert Desert

TIP

Check each area's detailed map in this guide to get a shopping list of what items you'll need to buy for that area's Moshlings.

Good luck, my marvelous Moshling collectors! Through this book, I'll be with you every step of the way.

Good hunting!
Buster Bumblechops

EXPLORING THE WOOLY WILDERNESS

It's really a jungle out there...but it's not just a jungle. There's also an ocean, a mountain range, some canyons, a few islands, a desert, farm land, forests, and city streets. Yes, there are a lot of things out there in the Wooly Wilderness. But Buster will take care of you! Here is my guide to the Wooly Wilderness, with all the Moshlings you can find in each area. Let's get this safari started!

TIP

For all of the areas, remember to keep checking back for new Moshlings or eggs to appear as you upgrade your zoo. And sometimes it takes a while for especially shy Moshlings to come out of hiding. If at first you don't find many Moshlings or eggs, upgrade your zoo habitats as much as you can. Then try, try again. And again. And again.

NOTE

Turn to the Monstropedia section of this book to find info on all the Moshlings and how to adopt them.

EXPLORING THE WOOLY WILDERNESS

Area 1: Whoop 'n' Holler Valley

Good old Whoop 'n' Holler Valley is a friendly place to start your search for Moshlings. Most of the critters in these parts aren't too shy about meeting a collector like you, so you should be able to nab a couple of Moshlings even on your first time passing through. Git along, little collector!

Who's hiding here?
Dipsy, Fifi, Flumpy, Honey, Humphrey, and Scamp

Area 2: Marshmallow Mountains

The Marshmallow Mountains in the Wooly Wilderness are certainly the most majestic marshmallow mountains you'll ever see. Don't get too distracted by their beauty, though! You're here on a mission, and there are plenty of Moshlings hiding in these hills.

Who's hiding here?
Angel, Ecto, Gingersnap, Lady Meowford, Pooky, and Waldo

Area 3: Wobbly Woods

Outside of the Wooly Wilderness, you can't find places like the Wobbly Woods, where you can watch TV right next to a lovely Moon Orchid garden. Now that seems downright civilized! Maybe I should try and do that when I get home.

Who's hiding here?
Big Bad Bill, Chop Chop, Doris, Jeepers, Prof. Purplex, and ShiShi

Area 4: Dessert Desert

If you're going to be wandering the Wilderness, the Dessert Desert is a tasty place to do it! Everywhere you look, a Foodie or its favorite items tempt you with sugary goodness. I like to spend an afternoon chilling out by the ice cream sandwiches under Coolio's umbrella.

Who's hiding here?
Cleo, Coolio, Cutie Pie, Mr. Snoodle, Oddie, Priscilla, and Wurley

Area 5: Potion Ocean

Ah, a trip to the beach. I can't wait to build sand castles and go swimming. And find lots of Fishies and some Birdies, of course. And maybe a Ninja. What fun is a beach without a Ninja?

Who's hiding here?
Cali, General Fuzuki, Peppy, Shelby, and Stanley

Area 6: Taki Taki Islands

Now this is the place to go for a party! DJ Quack plays his favorite funky music, and the islands only get more interesting as you explore. You might even see a (cardboard) celebrity! The islands are a tricky place to spot eggs; those tropical fruits hanging from the trees sure do look like eggs. Keep a sharp lookout for what you want!

Who's hiding here?
Blurp, Burnie, DJ Quack, Fumble, Holga, Liberty, and Rocky

Area 7: Kaleidoscope Canyons

If you like your lands mysterious, creepy, dark, and also very shiny, Kaleidoscope Canyons is the place for you! Moshlings who hide here enjoy glistening gems— or are scary Spookies who like to hide out in the dark. Either way, you'll be ready to seek them out!

Who's hiding here?
Gigi, Gurgle, Hansel, Kissy, Nipper, Purdy, and Squidge

Area 8: East Grumble

On the streets of East Grumble, you'll find a great mob of Moshlings frolicking in the rain. Put on your raincoat and galoshes, and get out there! It's probably just a little shower. Or a light sprinkle. Or...OK, it rains all the time here. But it's still a beautiful place to visit. There's even a sign that says so!

Who's hiding here?

Gabby, I.G.G.Y., McNulty, Mini Ben, Snookums, Sooki-Yaki, and White Fang

MONSTROPEDIA

BEASTIES

BURNIE

HABITAT:
Taki Taki Islands, on the volcanic island of Emberooze

Burnie's Egg

THE FIERY FRAZZLEDRAGON

Is it hot on this volcano or is it just...oh, it's just Burnie. These cheeky flying Beasties get into all kinds of sizzly mayhem, especially if they've been guzzling gasoline. (Talk about indigestion!) Gasoline is their favorite drink but it gives them terrible flaming hiccups. Fiery Frazzle-dragons love to char-grill silly sausages, but you'd better keep the fire extinguishers away from them or they'll think the party's over.

ULTRA RARE

ADOPTING BURNIE:

Burnie's barbecue is easy to spot in the field, but it's not so easy to get Burnie fired up to join your zoo. You'll need to get rid of the fire extinguisher, find the spit, find some gasoline, buy Burnie's favorite sausages...and then make sure your zoo is upgraded and leveled up enough to entice these finicky Fiery Frazzledragons to join you.

The perfect spot for a barbecue.

Habitat

Whoop 'n' Holler Valley,
in the Skedaddle
Prairie Ranch

HUMPHREY

THE SNORING
HICKOPOTUMUS

Humphrey's Egg

Yee-hah! Say howdy to the Moshlings that love digging, sowing,
milking, and mowing: the Snoring Hickopotumuses. If they're not
busy working the ranch, Snoring Hickos enjoy grabbing forty winks
under the shade of a wacky windmill. They also enjoy pickin' on
the banjo and mixing lazy daisy lemonade. Humphrey is a friendly
fellow...when he's awake, that is.

EXIT

Farm livin' is the life
for Humphrey.

ADOPTING HUMPHREY

To find Humphrey, go to Whoop 'n' Holler Valley and then...go east, young Moshling collector, go east. Humphrey's hiding out in the shade by the barn at the far right side of this area. Humphrey wants the simple things out of life: a banjo and a home on the range...or in your zoo, as long as you can get him some new twangy banjo strings. Head 'em up and move 'em out: you've got yourself a fine Hickopotumus!

JEEPERS

THE SNUGGLY TIGER CUB

HABITAT:
Wobbly Woods, in the Barmy Swami Jungle

Jeeper's Egg

These adorable Moshlings really have earned their stripes. That's because they spend ages painting them using inka-inka juice, squeezed from thumpkin seeds. Sadly the jungle is green, not yellow and stripy (but who wants to blend in, anyway)? In addition to decorating themselves, Snuggly Tiger Cubs love sharpening their claws and licking old swoonafish cans.

It's a jungle out here.

ADOPTING JEEPERS

Appeal to Jeepers's artistic side and you'll find a new (and nicely decorated) adoptee. Jeepers requires ground-up thumpkin seeds to make paint, plus painting supplies, but after he's got what he needs, you'll have a standout Moshling for your zoo.

SHISHI

HABITAT:
Wobbly Woods, in front of Gogglebox Gulch

THE SNEEZING PANDA

It always seems to be allergy season for Sneezing Pandas. These eyelash-fluttering Moshlings are obsessed with Monstrovision, but even that makes them sneeze. They will live anywhere as long as there is a big screen and comfy chair. When they're not glued to the screen, Sneezing Pandas are usually fiddling with magical eyedrops or scrunching up extra-soft tissues.

Shishi's Egg

ULTRA RARE

ADOPTING SHISHI

ShiShi requires the best entertainment and the finest tissues to be content. If you can also find some eyedrops, you'll have won the heart of this Sneezing Panda. Just make sure to dust frequently and be prepared with lots of tissues. (Only extra soft, please.)

The beautiful but not dust-free woods.

BIRDIES

moshi monsters MoshlingZo

HABITAT:

Potion Ocean, in the palm trees of Lush Lagoon

Tiki's Egg

TIKI

THE PILFERING TOUCAN

Colorful but crafty, Pilfering Toucans can't resist "borrowing" things from fellow Moshlings. Especially when those things are shiny. And when I say "borrow," I actually mean "steal" because this thieving flapper is one of the naughtiest pirates on the planet. When Pilfering Toucans aren't borrowing shiny stuff, they enjoy playing the squeezebox and drinking punch. (Contrary to popular belief, they do not seem to enjoy fruit-flavored breakfast cereals.)

ADOPTING TIKI

You've got to distract Pilfering Toucans from stealing some other Moshling's shiny stuff before they'll pay you any attention. Offering both a favorite toy and a super-rare Golden Rox gem will make Tiki take notice of you! Win Tiki over with a favorite beverage (hey, it gets hot in the tropics, playing with a squeezebox and collecting jewels).

Look, up in the sky—a Tiki bird! Admire your catch!
(Just don't stand underneath one for too long....)

HABITAT:

Taki Taki Islands, in the middle of Lake Neon Soup

DJ QUACK

DJ Quack's Egg

THE DISCO DUCKIE

You can tell by the way they waddle that Disco Duckies were born to boogie. Moving his feet to the disco beat, DJ Quack shakes a tail feather on the Taki Taki Islands, creating quite the bopping beach party. When they're not flapping around mirrorballs and dipping their beaks in glittery goop, these music-mad Moshlings are busy busting out new dance moves and slicking back their feathers with orange sauce.

ADOPTING DJ QUACK

There's no stopping a duck and its beat. Find and play that funky music for Disco Duckies and they'll want to waddle right into your zoo—but make sure they'll look good doing it. Find a shiny splatter of glittery goop and DJ Quack will ready to get the party started with your other Moshlings.

DJ Quack boogies to the beat on an island dancefloor.

PEPPY

HABITAT:
Potion Ocean, in the Frosty Pop Glacier

Peppy's Egg

THE STUNT PENGUIN

Peppy is one cool customer who loves popsicles, ice, and...bikes. Biker Penguins are rubbish at riding bikes (their feet don't reach the pedals), but these cool little guys are obsessed by two-wheels. So they slide along on their tummies making vroom-vroom noises and revving the air with their stumpy wings. Biker Penguins also scarf down a hundred pilchard popsicles a day!

ADOPTING PEPPY

Peppy's favorite things can all be found in his homeland, Potion Ocean. You won't find any frosty favorites in the tropics, however; head to Frosty Pop Glacier for a freezer and popsicle boxes! Place the popsicles in the freezer, and Peppy will think you're pretty cool.

Brrr...it's cold in here! Perfect popsicle weather for Peppy.

RARE

Prof Purplex's Egg

PROF PURPLEX

HABITAT:

Wobbly Woods,
in a tree hollow

RARE

THE OWL OF WISENESS

Owls of Wiseness are brainier than big brain pies with extra brain sprinkles. Able to digest an entire encyclopedia in ten seconds, these brainy birds have an appetite for knowledge—literally! Prof. Purplex enjoys art and literature, so hide your comics, because pictures are worth a thousand words. They also love the sound of plinky piano playing.

ADOPTING PROF PURPLEX

Adopting Prof. Purplex isn't perplexing; use your brain to meet Prof. Purplex's needs! Find the missing book from its collection and sheet music for the plinky piano, and you'll soon be able to add this Owl of Wiseness to you own Moshling collection. Brilliant!

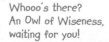

Whooo's there? An Owl of Wiseness, waiting for you!

DINOS

HABITAT:

Wobbly Woods, around the Garden Plot

Doris' Egg

DORIS

THE RUMMAGING PLOTAMUS

Unlike regular Plotamususes, Rummaging Plotamususes are obsessed with digging for fluffles, valuable toadstools that smell of licorice. These gentle little Moshlings also hibernate for much of the year. When they're not burrowing or snoozing, Plotamususes love gardening and gossiping. Doris would make a delightful addition to your zoo.

ADOPTING DORIS

Doris can't resist a beautiful garden, so make sure this one is in blooming great shape to attract her. Plant Moon Orchid seeds (you can find them near the garden) in the empty and filled-with-dead-flowers spots in the plot, water, and watch them grow! Doris is sure to stop by and admire your work. And remember, like all the Dinos, Doris won't appear unless your zoo's Dino house is open and upgraded.

Tiptoe through the Moon Orchid flowers.

HABITAT:

Kaleidoscope Canyons, in the glare of the Cadabra Flash

GURGLE

ULTRA RARE

Gurgle's Egg

THE PERFORMING FLAPPASAURUS

Performing Flappasauruses always have a trick up their wings. They usually go wrong, but it's best to applaud because these Dinos are very sensitive. If a magic routine goes badly, they've been known to burst into tears. What they really need is an automatic applause machine. And your attention and affection, of course.

ADOPTING GURGLE

Gurgle loves to perform—and it just so happens that there is a handy applause sign hanging around! Repair its broken bulbs and come prepared with tissues in case of a bad performance, and Gurgle will want to perform only at your zoo. And remember, like all the Dinos, Gurgle won't appear unless your zoo's Dino house is open and upgraded.

Where the lights shine bright... when they're not broken.

POOKY

THE POTTY PIPSQUEAK

HABITAT:

Marshmallow Mountains, in the Make-Believe Valley

Pooky's Egg

Don't be fooled. Playful Potty Pipsqueaks are not newly hatched Moshlings. They say they wear the odd headgear to protect themselves from Killer Canaries. Of course the Canaries only attack because the stolen eggshells belong to them! Potty Pipsqueaks steal them so that they can pretend to be spacemen. Pooky's dream is to be a space captain. Until then, he'll try to fly in your zoo.

ADOPTING POOKY

Pooky's dream of flying into space can come true with your help and a lot of imagination...oh, and stickers and a cardboard box. You can find the supplies in Pooky's area; you and Pooky will have to supply the imagination to turn that box into a spaceship. Blast off! And remember, like all the Dinos, Pooky won't appear unless your zoo's Dino house is open and upgraded.

Pooky's launch pad.

SNOOKUMS

HABITAT:

East Grumble, in the Sinky Hollow with yuckberry bushes

THE BABY
TUMTEEDUM

Hatched from mysterious marzipan eggs, Baby Tumteedums are always looking for someone to look after them and help keep them calm. And that's strange because they age in reverse, so babies are actually hundreds of years old. As well as being ancient, they eat two hundred yuckberries in a single day! These babies have big appetites.

ADOPTING SNOOKUMS

You'll need yuckberries to quiet this Baby Tumteedum's tummy, and then a quiet music CD to help this high-strung Dino relax. Helping Snookums chill out will make him want to snuggle up in your zoo. And remember, like all the Dinos, Snookums won't appear unless your zoo's Dino house is open and upgraded.

Snookum's Egg

Yummy yuckberries!

FISHIES

BLURP

THE BATTY
BUBBLEFISH

HABITAT:
Taki Taki Islands, in
the waters underneath
Fruit Falls

What a lovely spot for
a Fishie to live. I wonder
how Blurp got here? I
bet he wonders, too.

Batty Bubblefish spend most days swimming in
circles holding their breath. In fact, these sub-aquatic
Moshlings have got such terrible memories they can't
remember what it is they're supposed to have forgotten.
They like flip flops (even though they have fins, not feet).
Try to avoid upsetting a Batty Bubblefish, as they are
rather jumpy.

Blurp's Egg

ADOPTING BLURP

What Blurp really wants are some flip flops. What this forgetful Fishie really needs is a day planner to help him remember what he's supposed to be doing. Give Blurp both and you'll have no problem catching this Fishie!

HABITAT:

Potion Ocean, around the Coruscating Coral

Cali's Egg

CALI

THE VALLEY
MERMAID

Like, wow! There's something totally fishy going on here. When they're not freaking out over the latest koi band or chilling out in crates of ice, Valley Mermaids are hooking up fellow Moshlings. In fact, their hearts begin to flash whenever they sense romance. Funny they've never tried to set old Buster here up with someone....What-ever!

Some killer coral. That classic Cali.

ADOPTING CALI

So, do you, like, want to meet the raddest Moshling ever? Valley Mermaids might look totally high maintenance, but they're actually sweet. All they want is for that grodie rusty anchor to be so gone, and some ice so they can chill. Give Cali what she wants and she'll be majorly stoked to join your zoo.

RARE

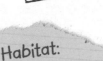

FUMBLE

THE ACROBATIC SEA STAR

Habitat:
Taki Taki Islands, on the Bleurgh Lagoon Reef

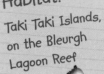

Acrobatic SeaStars are willing to risk all five limbs when performing stunts...fortunately for them, they can pretty easily get their limbs back in working order! When they're not boinging along the seabed performing death-defying stunts to rock music, or bungee-ing from towering coral formations, Acrobatic SeaStars spend most days gluing their pointy bits back on. In fact they're the clumsiest Moshlings in town, but they still hate safety nets.

ADOPTING FUMBLE

Fumble needs your help to support his stunts. This means being ready for the likely outcome: a slightly battered SeaStar. Have bandages on hand for Fumble's appendages, and find the safety net and rock music CD. Fumble will be ready to rock and you'll be ready to fix him up again.

Go to the lagoon to watch Fumble's five legs perform acrobatic feats.

Fumble's Egg

HABITAT:

Potion Ocean, in the Reggae Reef

STANLEY

THE SONGFUL SEAHORSE

Stanley's Egg

Although very cute, Songful SeaHorses are also incredibly annoying, because they can't stop whistling awful show tunes at ear-splitting volume. Experts believe they're trying to attract other SeaHorses but no one can stay long enough to find out. They love sea oats (and, apparently, show tunes).

ADOPTING STANLEY

Plug your ears (or otherwise turn down the volume) and prepare to meet one of the cutest seahorses you'll ever see in the sea. Stanley's adorableness makes up for his whistling habit. Give him some sea oats to eat (you can't whistle with your mouth full, right?) and a CD on his radio and you'll have one happy Songful SeaHorse.

Watch for Stanley swimming in shallow water.

FLUFFIES

HABITAT:

Whoop 'n' Holler Valley, in the Meringue Meadow under Vanilla Pod trees

Dipsy's Egg

DIPSY

THE DINKY DREAMCLOUD

Vanilla Pod trees in Meringue Meadow— yum! No wonder Dipsy is hungry for something sweet.

Dinky Dreamclouds dream of one day becoming Ginormous Dreamclouds, but they are far too teeny for that important job. That's why they flutter and flap about all day, making cute noises and admiring their eyelashes. They like marmalade with bits and dislike modern dance. Dipsy might look soft and puffy, but Dinky Dreamclouds do not like soft music.

ADOPTING DIPSY

Dipsy just might be the first Moshling to join your zoo. (Awww, thanks, Dipsy!) The only item you're given to start your expedition is a jar of marmalade, which happens to be Dipsy's favorite! This Dinky Dreamcloud will get your zoo off to a sweet and cuddly start.

HABITAT:

Whoop 'n' Holler Valley, in the Cotton Clump plantation

FLUMPY

Flumpy's Egg

THE PLUFF

Pluffs are the most chilled out of all the Moshlings. You'll see them strolling about, arms dangling, huge grins on their faces. If you want to chillax, then look no further. About the only thing that can make them sad is clutter, but show them a well-polished chair and all is well. Merely looking at Flumpy is likely to make you feel like you've just gotten a big hug from a cottonball.

A perfectly polished rocking chair, surrounded by pink cottonballs, overlooking Lilypad Lake...I feel relaxed already.

ADOPTING FLUMPY

Pluffs are the most mellow of all Moshlings, but they can't relax amidst a mess. Clear Flumpy's area from the clutter that's scattered around the ground, and polish that nice wooden chair for Flumpy to stretch out on. He'll be so blissed out, he'll happily join your zoo. (Even though he looks so cottony soft, don't try to use *him* to polish that chair. Flumpy might not be so laid-back about being used as a cleaning cloth...even if he does look so perfect for the job....)

HONEY

Honey's Egg

HABITAT:
Whoop 'n' Holler
Valley, near
Pawberry Fields

THE FUNNY BUNNY

When they're not busy texting jokes to their friends, Funny Bunnies can be found yacking about carrot cake. These cottontailed cuties have one floppy ear. Experts think this is caused by listening to silly ringtones all day. They love naffodils, but hate lukewarm nincomsoup. Keep an ear out for ringing cell phones.

I could just look at
Pawberry Fields forever.

ADOPTING HONEY

While most Bunnies would appreciate flowers and cake, you'll win Honey over completely with these offerings! Honey will put her calls on hold if you give her naffodil flowers in a vase, followed up with her favorite carrot cake. Hop to it!

RARE

I.G.G.Y

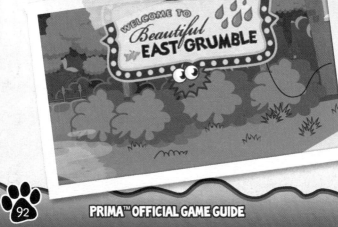

HABITAT:
East Grumble,
hiding in the hedges

I.G.G.Y's Egg

THE PIXEL-MUNCHING SNAFFLER

The Pixel-Munching Snaffler Moshlings look innocent enough, but the second they spot a pointy arrow, it's history. Experts believe they find cursors really annoying, like flies flittering around their heads. They enjoy power surges and tickly pickles, but have a tendency to get stuck in hedges. Try to avoid power surges around them.

WELCOME TO *Beautiful* EAST GRUMBLE

ULTRA RARE

ADOPTING I.G.G.Y

Let old Bumblechops point you in the right direction: to adopt I.G.G.Y., you're going to need to find an errant arrow and put it in its place, or I.G.G.Y. will never pay any attention to you. Get the billboard's electronics working again, and then offer I.G.G.Y. a tickly pickle. He'll be so excited to eat it, he won't have any appetite for that arrow you found.

I.G.G.Y. hides in the hedges, waiting for delicious arrows or pickles to happen by.

FOODIES

COOLIO

HABITAT:

Dessert Desert, in the frozen Knickerbocker Nook

Coolio's Egg

THE MAGICAL SPARKLEPOP

It sounds a tad absurd, but these tubby Moshlings are enchanted. Whenever they need to chill, glittery sparks zing around their slurpy swirls. Even so, they try to stay out of the sun because Magical Sparklepops go all gloopy if it gets too hot. They love scarfing down whackcurrant sauce and crushed nuts.

ADOPTING COOLIO

You'll find Coolio keeping his cool in the frosty regions of the Dessert Desert. Prevent a major meltdown by giving him some shade: replace the broken umbrella spring. Then offer his favorite toppings, crushed nuts and whackcurrant sauce, to sweeten the deal.

Staying cool in the desert.

RARE

HABITAT:

Dessert Desert, atop Cutie Pie Canyon on Ramekin Plain

Cutie Pie's Egg

CUTIE PIE

THE WHEELIE YUMYUM

Talk about a sugar rush! These scrumptilicious Moshlings move like lightning, but so would you if you had turbo-charged sprinkles and a woowoo-ing cherry on your head. Wheelie YumYums are often forced to flee from hungry predators. (They do look good enough to eat....) Follow the trail and you might find one filling up with a few gallons of cocoa.

ULTRA RARE

Living off of cocoa fuel is the cherry on top of a sweet life for Cutie Pie.

ADOPTING CUTIE PIE

This is one high-energy Moshling. Cutie Pie needs lots of sugary fuel to keep his energy up for playing tag and racing around the desert. Help him get his sugar rush by fixing the broken cocoa pump and he'll be ready to race back to your zoo. Sweet!

HANSEL

THE PSYCHO
GINGERBOY

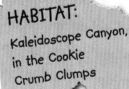

HABITAT:
Kaleidoscope Canyon,
in the Cookie
Crumb Clumps

Hansel's Egg

He's out of the pan and ready for action. Don't
be fooled by the fancy frosting and biscuity
cuteness—Psycho Gingerboys are naughty trouble-
makers. When they're not stealing sweets, they like
hanging around on street corners and tripping up
passers-by. Thankfully, Psycho Gingerboys are easy
to catch with liquorice nets and custard baths.

ADOPTING HANSEL

You don't need to follow a trail of breadcrumbs to find Hansel; just follow these tips! Hansel might want you to think you can't catch him, but the secret for getting him is to *not* run, run as fast as you can. If you get him to stay in one place, you've got him. Tempt Hansel with a custard-filled tub, and then drop the liquorice net on him for an especially delicious capture.

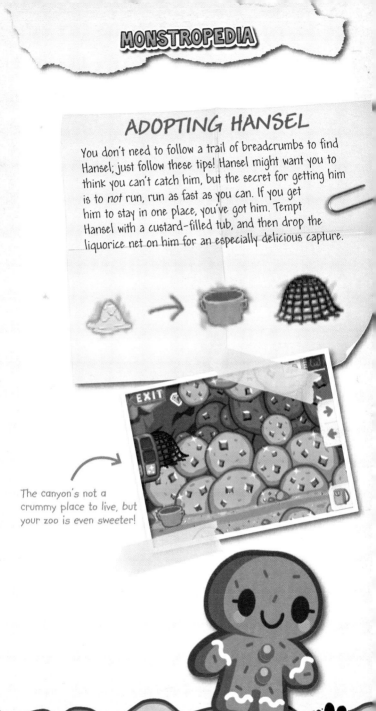

The canyon's not a crummy place to live, but your zoo is even sweeter!

ODDIE

Oddie's Egg

HABITAT:
Dessert Desert, in the Boiling Oil Swamp

THE SWEET RINGY THINGY

Oddie loves to dunk himself into a nice vat of boiling oil.

With their doughy bodies and gloopy icing, Ringy Thingies look exceedingly delicious. If you're wondering how a bunch of sticky doughnutters ever became living Moshlings, don't. It will only make your brain ache. Just know that they love food with lots of O's and hate purple sprouting broccoli.

ULTRA RARE

ADOPTING ODDIE

Broccoli belongs nowhere near a delightful dessert like Oddie. Make sure that any vegetables are out of sight, and get ready for a sugar overload. This Sweet Ringy Thingy desires lots and lots of sprinkles. But the icing on the cake for Oddie is deep-fried OoblaDoobla.

KITTIES

GINGERSNAP

THE WHINGER CAT

Moaning, lazy, and strangely charming, Whinger Cats are said to be really good at fixing things. Nobody knows if it's true because they never bother showing up. Maybe it's because they're busy waiting for other things, like bedtime and dinnertime. They enjoy hammocks, and hate work, work, and work.

Gingersnap thinks this looks like a purrrfect spot for a nap.

Gingersnap's Egg

ADOPTING GINGERSNAP

What's that? Gingersnap is awake?! Oh, I see...his hammock is broken. Repair Gingersnap's favorite spot for a catnap and he'll follow you home. If he can stay awake. Yawwwn!

HABITAT:

Marshmallow Mountains, in
the High & Mighty Mountains

LADY MEOWFORD

THE PRETTY KITTY

Pretty Kitties are frightfully sweet but a bit annoying.
It's because these cute Moshlings are always right about
everything. Pretty Kitties are very musical and have incredibly
high-pitched singing voices. They can't stand common kitty
toys or balls of string, but are quite fond of harp music.

Lady Meowford's Egg

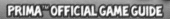

ADOPTING LADY MEOWFORD

Remove any toys a regular housecat would enjoy; that ball of string must be disposed of at once. Next, locate Lady Meowford's sheet music, and, since actual harpists aren't common in Marshmallow Mountains, play a harp music CD. It's mewsic to her ears! Lady Meowford will graciously accept your invitiation to join your residence for kitties.

Lady Meowford looks down on the world from the High & Mighty Mountains.

PURDY

HABITAT:
Kaleidoscope Canyons, in the Candy Cane Caverns

THE TUBBY
HUGGISHI

A pretty place
for Purdy.

Tubby Huggishis are huggable Moshlings that spend most days preening and lounging about eating piles of pastry. That's why most of them are a little on the large side. When not devouring cakes, these shaggy felines enjoy writing advice columns for the Moshling News and dipping their paws in syrup.

ADOPTING PURDY

Purdy needs to meet her newspaper's deadline and mail in her advice column! Help her complete her task so she can celebrate with a pastry. Find her a stamp, find her a pastry, and you will find yourself with one content (but sticky) kitty.

Purdy's Egg

THE TABBY NERDICAT

HABITAT:
Marshmallow Mountains, in the Honeycomb Foothills

A Tabby Nerdicat can tell you the square root of a banana in a flash, but thinks cool means sitting in a bucket of ice. They spend most of their time arguing over comics and playing Oubliettes and Ogres. Finding Tabby Nerdicats is harder than reverse algebra, but they seem to like toffee nachos.

1 Nerdicat + 1 stack of comic books = 1 more Moshling in your zoo

Waldo's Egg

RARE

ADOPTING WALDO

Waldo will appreciate the skills of an intelligent zookeeper such as yourself. Be smart in your approach, and this Nerdicat will be quick to join your zoo. Give Waldo his entertainment essentials (comic books, of course) to net you one clever cat.

NINJAS

HABITAT:

Wobbly Woods, by the
Sniggerton Trees

CHOP CHOP

THE CHEEKY CHIMP

Cheeky Chimps are part-time ninjas and full-time jokers. They leave a trail of banana skins wherever they go. In fact these playful primates don't know when to stop. And that can be pretty funny--unless the joke's on you. Watch out or you could end up with a faceful of custard pie and a rubber chicken in your soup. (Maybe I've been out in the Wooly Wilderness too long, but that doesn't sound half bad!)

ADOPTING CHOP CHOP

To adopt Chop Chop, you'll need to find items that
ap-*peel* to him. Chop Chop loves music. Play his favorite
CD (you can find it near him) and offer up a treat any
Cheeky Chimp can't resist: a banana peel. Chop Chop will
soon be planning hilarious high jinks in your zoo.
And remember, like all the Ninjas, Chop Chop
won't appear unless your zoo's Ninja house is open
and upgraded.

Chop Chop's Egg

Chop Chop. Who's there?
Banana peel!

GENERAL FUZUKI

HABITAT:

Potion Ocean, in
Chilly Bot State Park

THE WARRIOR
WOMBAT

ULTRA RARE

Warrior Wombats guard shiny stuff, because they don't need any sleep. Or do they? New research shows that their open eyes are actually cake tins welded to their funny hats. This allows them to take forty winks on the sly.

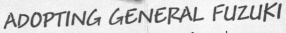

General Fuzuki's Egg

Ice is nice for
General Fuzuki.

ADOPTING GENERAL FUZUKI

General Fuzuki knows the importance of a good nap...or
two, or three, or four good naps! Help him wake up with
his alarm clock and return his shiny treasure. Once he
sees how well you can take care of him, he'll want to
snooze in your zoo for good. And remember, like all
the Ninjas, General Fuzuki won't appear unless your zoo's
Ninja house is open and upgraded.

SHELBY

HABITAT:
Potion Ocean, by the Wailing Wharf of Groan Bay

Shelby's Egg

THE SLAPSTICK TORTOISE

Slapstick Tortoises are highly trained. Unfortunately, whoever trained them was rubbish because they're only good at falling over and ending belly-side up. If they would train rather than watch kung fu movies, brush their teeth with toffee, and buff their shells, they might not be so useless. They sure are cute, though.

ADOPTING SHELBY

Shelby has gotten all dirty from practicing kung fu! Find extra soft tissues so he can shine up his shell. Then track down a tube of toffee toothpaste. Slapstick Tortoises love this sticky stuff! Just take it from me, don't try to use it yourself. You won't get unstuck for days. And remember, like all the Ninjas, Shelby won't appear unless your zoo's Ninja house is open and upgraded.

Under the boardwalk, down by the sea, is where Shelby might be.

SOOKI-YAKI

HABITAT:
East Grumble, on the
Dripping Drainpipes

THE CAPED ASSASSIN

Caped Assassins are not as good at sneaking around as they think they are. Don't laugh, because these agile little Moshlings have the ability to vanish and re-appear in an instant. The problem is they can't control their power, especially when frightened and pop up where they shouldn't. Sudden cuteness popping up in front of you can give you a scare!

Mysterious drainpipes, Sooki-Yaki's favorite places to prowl.

Sooki-Yaki's Egg

ADOPTING SOOKI-YAKI

Sooki-Yaki hides in the shadows of East Grumble. Light a firecracker to get her attention! Unfortunately, Sooki-Yaki gets startled by firecrackers, and she'll need a bandage after falling from her hiding place. She'll be fine, and she'll be happy to join your zoo. And remember, like all the Ninjas, Sooki-Yaki won't appear unless your zoo's Ninja house is open and upgraded.

PONIES

ANGEL

THE SKYPONY

HABITAT:

Marshmallow
Mountain, in
Cloud Nine

This little SkyPony
thinks the world is a
lovely place.

Until recently, Angel SkyPonies were mentioned only in Moshi
legend. But that was before a whole herd appeared on a pink
cloud, high above Mount Sillimanjaro. These heavenly creatures
rarely visit ground level, but when they do, they enjoy listening
to harp music and eating cottony things that are soft and fluffy.
They also enjoy soft and fluffy blankets to snuggle with when
sleeping. (But I don't think they eat their blankets.)

Angel's Egg

ADOPTING ANGEL

Flying around the sky makes a SkyPony hungry! Feed Angel fluffy cotton candy (buy it from the store), and she'll be ready for...a nap. (Sugar doesn't seem to have the same effect on Moshlings that it has on me.) Give her a fluffy blanket, and maybe she'll even let you ride her back to the zoo! (OK, she won't do that. But she will join your zoo.)

HABITAT:

Kaleidoscope Canyon, in the Gem Grotto

Gigi's Egg

THE MAGICAL MULE

Magical Mules are descended from enchanted carousel horses. They can even create rainbows! That's why they trot along humming fairground tunes and gliding up and down as if still attached to a merry-go-round. Magical Mules eat wild fluttercups and cotton candy and love marimba music.

ADOPTING GIGI

To get Gigi to gallop to your zoo, make sure the Ponies area is upgraded and looking good. This Magical Mule has sky-high standards. You'll win her over with her festive favorites: playing a marimba music CD, and offering fluttercups and cotton candy. She won't say *neigh* to that!

Gigi waltzes around the gems.

ULTRA RARE

MR. SNOODLE

THE SILLY SNUFFLER

HABITAT:

Dessert Desert, by Franzipan Farm

Silly Snufflers are some of the sleepiest, snuffliest Moshlings around. Whenever they amble by looking for pumpernickel breadcrumbs, monsters just yawn and fall asleep. By the time a monster has woken up, the Snufflers have managed to (slowly) get away. They love soft music, but no jazz, please!

Mr. Snoodle's Egg

ADOPTING MR. SNOODLE

Yaaawn! Oh, excuse me! I must be having a sugar crash from spending too much time in the Dessert Desert. Then again, it's probably from Mr. Snoodle. He has that effect on people and monsters. Mr. Snoodle wants soft music and pumpernickle bread crumbs. I recommend ear plugs, so you don't doze off while listening to that soft music!

A delicious spot for a nap.

RARE

PRISCILLA

HABITAT:

Dessert Desert,
near Gluey Gulch

THE PRINCESS PONY

Rumoured to be descended from royalty, Princess Ponies are always fiddling with their tiaras, waving their hooves at passers-by, and searching for sparkly candy apples. If their regal routines fail to impress, prepare to be astounded because they can make their manes and tails change color. Now that is royally cool!

A likely spot to find Priscilla, Princess Pony of the Dessert Desert.

ADOPTING PRISCILLA

A Princess Pony's got to make sure she has a crown at all times. Present her with her spare crown you've found, and then trot out a sparkly candy-coated apple. Priscilla will want to make your zoo her new kingdom. (Perhaps she can teach the other Ponies to curtsy.)

Priscilla's Egg

PUPPIES

HABITAT:

Whoop 'n' Holler Valley by the Pink and Fluffy Forest

FIFI

Fifi's Egg

THE OOCHIE POOCHIE

Oochie Poochies are sweet, fluffy, and totally obsessed with the finer things in life, from fancy food to the very latest fur styles. When they're not sipping lemonade or making sure all the napkins are perfectly ironed, these Moshlings like nibbling on the cotton candy on the end of their tails. Yum!

Only fluffy trees will do for Fifi!

ADOPTING FIFI

Fifi might seem high maintenance, but she's one of the friendliest Moshlings around. She'll wander out of hiding quickly, but will scamper away just as fast unless you iron her cloth napkins!

HABITAT:

East Grumble, by the Sherlock Home

McNulty's Egg

MCNULTY

THE UNDERCOVER YAPYAP

Undercover YapYaps are nosy puppies that love sniffing out secrets and investigating secret notes...or is that a grocery list? These cute snoops are also masters of disguise. The only way to be sure you're dealing with one is to check out their paw prints, which is why they always try to erase them.

McNulty walks the mean streets, collecting clues.

138

ADOPTING McNULTY

How to nab McNulty? Elementary, my dear Moshling collector: give him the goods. This is top secret intel, but between you and me, a towel will do the trick to help him keep his cover. In the shadowy streets of East Grumble, McNulty has a hard time reading secret messages. Hand over the magnifying glass and you'll have this case all locked up.

SCAMP

HABITAT:

Whoop 'n' Holler Valley, near Lilypad Lake

THE FROGGIE DOGGIE

Lilypad Lake is a good swimming spot... if you're a frog.

Why would a cute little puppy want to boing around wearing a rubbery frog suit? Alas, Froggie Doggies are too busy yelling "ribbit" to answer silly questions. These dogs think they're frogs so they often gather at Lilypad Lake—a bad idea, since they can't swim. (Anybody know how to doggie paddle?)

ULTRA RARE

Scamp's Egg

ADOPTING SCAMP

Scamp needs a towel to dry off after a dip in the water. But before any of that, you must remove the lilypads that are clogging up Lilypad Lake. A Puppy hardly has room to do laps with all those lilypads floating around!

WHITE FANG

RARE

THE MUSKY HUSKY

HABITAT:

East Grumble, near the Dank Dumpsters

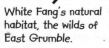
White Fang's natural habitat, the wilds of East Grumble.

Musky Huskies will do anything for a bite to eat. They've been spotted rummaging through dumpsters searching for doggie bags and old bones. Maybe that's why they look so scruffy. Take care if you pet one of these greedy, mucky pups—it might bite off your fingers...or run away. Fortunately, you are an expert Puppy catcher.

142

ADOPTING WHITE FANG

White Fang hunts in dumpsters for food, any kind of food, as long as it keeps him full. It's not as bad as "eat or be eaten" out here in East Grumble; for White Fang, the options are more like "eat or...eat some more." He won't have to go dumpster diving tonight: find him a bone and a doggie bag, and White Fang will be happy to leave the call of the Wilderness behind.

White Fang's Egg

SPOOKIES

HABITAT:

Wobbly Woods, in the Gombala Gombala Jungle

ULTRA RARE

BIG BAD BILL

THE WOOLLY BLUE HOODOO

Wooly Blue Hoodoos are wise old Moshlings who know everything about lotions, potions, hexes, and spells. But Woolly Blue Hoodoos are not as brave as most of their patients—they're scared of teaspoons! A heaping serving of bald peaches and some deep fried oobladoobla will help that! (Although I must say, ol' Buster here is afraid of food stuffed inside of other food. I would stay away from that oobladoobla!)

The jungle is littered with terrifying teaspoons.

EXIT

Big Bad Bill's Egg

ADOPTING BIG BAD BILL

Big Bad Bill isn't really bad at all. He's probably just scared silly because there seem to be a lot of teaspoons in the Gombala Gombala Jungle. Remove the frightening flatware for him. Next, serve up those non-fuzzy peaches he likes so much, followed by a hefty portion of deep fried oobladoobla, and Big Bad Bill will be a Big Happy Moshling!

RARE

ECTO

HABITAT:
Marshmallow Mountain, near the ClothEar Cloud Formation

THE FANCY
BANSHEE

Don't be afraid, Fancy Banshees are the friendliest of Moshlings. But don't touch one because their creepy glowing capes are made of electrified wobble-plasma which turns things inside-out! These Moshlings float around collecting Rox dust. They dislike being out in the sun and anyone called Ichabod.

PRIMA™ OFFICIAL GAME GUIDE

ADOPTING ECTO

Ecto's hangout is already well stocked with the items you need to attract him; you just need to put them all together. Ecto is afraid of strong sunlight, so fix his umbrella with a new spring to make shade. (Almost as good as hiding in the dark.) Open the treasure box, and Ecto will want to scream with joy at the sight of so much mysterious Rox dust.

A relaxing spot to hide from the sun.

Ecto's Egg

KISSY

THE BABY
GHOST

HABITAT:

Kaleidoscope Canyon,
in the Okay-ish Lands

There's something
Spooky in this
neighborhood.

It's hard being scary when you're as cute as a Baby Ghost.
These supernatural Moshlings are more interested in glittery
goop, toys, fluffy poodles, and pink ribbons than sneaking
around frightening Moshi Monsters. If you do see a Baby Ghost,
try not to breathe near it or it might evaporate. Trust me, I've
done it before. Ol' Buster is a bit of a Baby Ghost, um, buster.

Kissy's Egg

ADOPTING KISSY

Like most babies, all Kissy really wants is some glittery goop and a pink ribbon for her toy poodle. Get her the goods, and hold your breath. She'll gladly float on over to your zoo, as long as you don't make her evaporate!

HABITAT:

Kaleidoscope Canyons, in the Crazy Caves of Fang-Ten Valley

Squidge's Egg

SQUIDGE

THE FURRY HEEBEE

Furry Heebees are greedy bloodsuckers that flutter around at night hunting for juicy victims, but they'll settle for a nice mug of instant toe-mato soup with plenty of garlicky croutons. Oh yes, they also love capes and crying "mwah-ha-ha!" It's enough to give you goosebumps!

ADOPTING SQUIDGE

These Crazy Caves sure are cold...no wonder we've got goosebumps. Squidge needs to warm up, too. (Sure, he's furry, but it's still cold in here!) Hand this Heebee a long cape and some warm toe-mato soup. Squidge will warm up to you! Just don't let him stay too close to you. He can get a bit nippy.

Goosebump-inducing caves.

TECHIES

GABBY

THE MINI MOSHIFONE

HABITAT:

East Grumble, near Voltage Vaults

Whether they're flashing up funny messages, chatting to friends, playing games, or composing new ringtones, these high-tech dinga-linging Moshlings are always on hand to help conduct endless chit-chats. Just prod their fancy touchscreens and holler. It's for you!

ADOPTING GABBY

Gabby can't gab without being charged up! Locate Gabby's charger so she can tell her Moshling friends that she's working again. But how can she call her new friend Honey if she can't find her number? You can help with that, too. Give her Honey's digits and Gabby's next convo will be all about your awesome zoo. And remember, like all the Techies, Gabby won't appear unless your zoo's Techie house is open and upgraded.

This part of town is electrifying!

Gabby's Egg

HOLGA

HABITAT:
Taki Taki Islands,
on Shutter Island

THE HAPPY SNAPPY

Say cheese and strike a pose because Happy Snappies are the Moshlings that just love taking photos, especially if there's a famous monster in town. Get the picture? You will because they can't resist handing out snaps to everyone they meet. They love towering tripods and hot celebrities.

Holga's Egg

Hmm...no celebrities around here. Looks like you'd better bring one.

ADOPTING HOLGA

Find Holga's tripod's missing leg and she'll be ready for a celebrity sighting. It's up to you to provide the celebrity— or in this case, a cardboard cutout of one. You must buy the cardboard celebrity in Horrods, and it costs 2,000 Rox. (Even cardboard celebrities command high prices.) But Holga will be so happy! And remember, like all the Techies, Holga won't appear unless your zoo's Techie house is open and upgraded.

NIPPER

ULTRA RARE

HABITAT:
Kaleidoscope Canyons,
in Quivering Quarry

THE TITCHY
TRUNDLEBOT

TrundleBots can pluck Rox from the highest trees, trundle
across bumpy surfaces, and warn Monsters of falling
boulders. It's easy thanks to their stretchy-flexi arms and
caterpillar-clad tootsies. They love construction site safety
and are always up for a game of basketball.

ADOPTING NIPPER

It's always safety first for Nipper! The TrundleBot makes it his mission to keep all Moshlings (and their collectors) safe, especially around construction sites. You'll need a hardhat and a sign about nearby falling rocks. And remember, like all the Techies, Nipper won't appear unless your zoo's Techie house is open and upgraded.

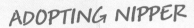

Be on the lookout here for Nipper— and falling rocks!

Nipper's Egg

Wurley's Egg

WURLEY

HABITAT:

Dessert Desert, over Nuttanbolt Lake

THE TWIRLY TIDDLYCOPTER

Thanks to their motory-rotory headgear, these tin-skinned flying Moshlings are always in demand, especially when they are transporting precious thingies. As they wokka-wokka through the clouds, Tiddlycopters love humming classical music, munching on windsocks dipped in oil, and guzzling gasoline.

Look, up in the sky! It's a Moshling!

ULTRA RARE

ADOPTING WURLEY

It's not my cup of tea, but Wurley's favorite treat is an oil-soaked windsock. Yes, to eat. Help him out and he'll be flying high—just make sure to keep him away from any open flames! And remember, like all the Techies, Wurley won't appear unless your zoo's Techie house is open and upgraded.

WORLDIES

HABITAT:

Dessert Desert, on the
Banks of River Smile

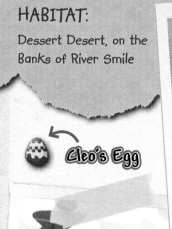

Cleo's Egg

CLEO

THE PRETTY
PYRAMID

Experts thought Pretty Pyramids were extinct until a
sandstorm blew away a desert dune, revealing the lost
valley of iSissi. Apart from making big sand castles,
these Moshlings spend their days searching for lost
treasure. They also love precious stones (especially Rox)
and anything made of gold.

ADOPTING CLEO

Cleo is on the hunt for treasure, and a map will guide her straight to it. She loves shiny stones and gold objects, so a sparkly golden Rox gem is the best treasure of all! But how can she collect treasure and build those famous sandcastles? A bucket is just what she needs! And remember, like all the Worldies, Cleo won't appear unless your zoo's Worldie house is open and upgraded.

There's room for a lot of sandcastles here.

ULTRA RARE

LIBERTY

HABITAT:

Taki Taki Islands,
on Divinity Island

Liberty's Egg

THE HAPPY STATUE

With an ice cream in one hand and a wish list in the other, Happy Statues believe in having fun, playing games, and making dream books. It's not that they are greedy, they just adore wishing for yummy treats, cool clothes, and twinkly trinkets. Just don't let them run out of batteries. Liberty requires a lot of energy!

Divinity Island, with Liberty
and ice cream cones for all.

RARE

ADOPTING LIBERTY

Chasing after Liberty is what this old Moshling collector calls the pursuit of happiness! Keep Liberty alive with some batteries. After she's come to life, help her find her dream book and the pictures that go in it. Liberty can't lose her dreams! And remember, like all the Worldies, Liberty won't appear unless your zoo's Worldie house is open and upgraded.

MINI BEN

THE TEENY TICKTOCK

HABITAT:
East Grumble, near
Westmonster Abbey

Mini Ben's Egg

Teeny TickTocks love chiming on the hour, every hour.
These terribly old-fashioned chaps enjoy waxing their
bushy moustaches, nibbling cucumber sandwiches, and
asking everyone the time. Well, have you ever tried
looking at a clock that's on top of your head?
It's harder than you think!

ADOPTING MINI BEN

Mini Ben is a nice old clock who really needs a hand: First bring him a wristwatch, so he can finally tell the time for himself. Splendid! Next, help Mini Ben by finding his favorite moustache wax; he'll be looking quite dashing in no time. When it's tea time, bring a basket full of tiny sandwiches. Smashing! Mini Ben will be jolly glad to have met you! And remember, like all the Worldies, Mini Ben won't appear unless your zoo's Worldie house is open and upgraded.

The boo-tiful Westmonster Alley.

ULTRA RARE

ROCKY

HABITAT:

Taki Taki Islands, in the Rocky Ruins of Beaster Island

THE BABY BLOCKHEAD

One rockin' island.

These heavyweight Moshlings are very strong—hardly surprising as they're solid rock (like their favorite music!). The trouble is, they don't know their own strength and often break things by accident, especially their stuffed bunny toys and fingers when they shake hands.

RARE

Rocky's Egg

ADOPTING ROCKY

Rocky sure is a lovable blockhead. All Rocky really wants is to snuggle up with his fuzzy bunny toy, but he's crushed that he's accidentally broken it again! Fortunately, you've found its bits and pieces scattered across Beaster Island. Stitch his bunny back together, and tell him how nice it will be to live at your zoo. He can even bring his bunny. And remember, like all the Worldie Rocky won't appear unless your zoo's Worldie house is open and upgraded.

MASTERING THE MINI-GAMES

All zookeepers must take care of their critters, but in your zoo, you also get to play games with yours! You can play mini-games with the Moshlings in your zoo to feed them, bathe them, and train them. As you play the training mini-games, you'll earn lots of Rox, but you'll also level up your Moshlings to increase their performance in the most important Moshling competition around: the Ulti-Moshling Contest!

Food Challenge

Moshlings are ready to chow down!

SERVED 2
GOAL 7
BONUS 5 0
CHANCES

This game is all about really fast food. Your job is to put together a disgustingly delicious combination of plate color, food, syrup, and a topping, and feed it to each Moshling before the timer runs out! You must match the meal you serve to the picture that shows what each Moshling wants.

A hungry crowd of Moshlings can get mighty impatient.

There are two ways you can get to the Food Challenge mini-game: by click on a Moshling in your zoo, or through the Glormatorium. If you want to earn Rox and feed a certain Moshling at the same time, go to your zoo, click on a Moshling, and choose the Food Challenge icon. Your Moshling's hunger status will improve after successfully playing this game! If you play by going through the Glormatorium, you'll earn Rox and your zoo level will go up, but you won't benefit any one Moshling's hunger status.

Start from the bottom up: plate first, then food item, then syrup, and then a topping. Remember to drag your dish to the Moshling to feed it, or it won't count! If you get behind, you might want to skip over one Moshling whose time is almost up and move ahead to the next in line to get back on track. You have five chances to skip over Moshlings before your game's over, and you'll get 25 Rox for each Moshling you feed. Moshlings will eat a plate of food that isn't theirs (they must really be hungry!), and they'll leave after eating, but you won't get credit for feeding that Moshling.

Bathing

Rub-a-dub-dub, Moshlings in the tub! All that playing around in the Wooly Wilderness and roughhousing in the zoo can really make a Moshling dirty. Clean your Moshling by matching the soap color to each Moshling, dragging it over to the Moshling, and repeat, until the graphic changes to the next step: the scrub brush. Keep dragging the scrub brush until it changes to a shower, and then the towel. Wash, rinse, and repeat for all the Moshlings in your tub!

Splish splash, one Moshling in the bath.

These Moshlings don't want to stay in the tub too long, though; you've got to be quick, before they wander away! You've got five chances (represented by the hearts) to lose Moshlings before your game's over and the time runs out. You'll get 10 Rox for each Moshling you get squeaky clean!

You've got a full pool!

MASTERING THE MINI-GAMES

Just like the Food Challenge, there are two ways you can get to the Bathing mini-game: by clicking on a Moshling in your zoo, or through the Glormatorium. If you want to earn Rox and bathe a certain Moshling at the same time, go to your zoo, click on a Moshling, and choose the Bathing icon. Your Moshling's cleanliness level will improve after successfully playing this game! If you play by going through the Glormatorium, your Moshlings' cleanliness will improve even more (although slightly). You'll also earn Rox and your zoo level will increase.

NOTE

Moshling Babies Mini-Game

The cutest mini-game around is the Moshling babies game! To play, you can visit my place, Buster's Baby Care Center, or select any baby Moshling in your zoo and click on the nursery icon. The game sends you to the nursery and gives you four Moshling babies to comfort; you need to drag the object each baby wants to the baby, and let it get its fill of cuddling to earn 10 Rox per baby. This game might not bring in lots of Rox or send your training levels soaring, but those baby Moshlings are irresistible!

Speedy Feats

Choose your Moshling and get ready to race! Move your Moshlings by touching the screen, making them hop, swim, fly, or run for Rox. You'll not only collect loads of Rox, but you'll be training your chosen Moshling to prepare for the Ulti-Moshling Contest. You can also make your Moshlings happy by racing and training. You don't *have* to feed them or wash them (sorry, Moshlings), but you must train them with races and Rapid Matches/Quik Wits to do well in the Ulti-Moshling Contest. As you level up your Moshlings, the races will become harder.

OK, Fifi...on your mark...
get set...

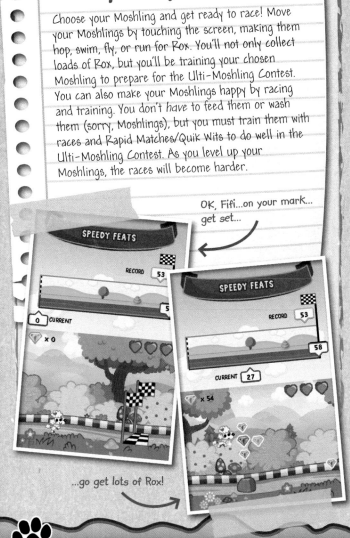

...go get lots of Rox!

Moshlings race by land, sea, and air.

The races are huge Rox-grabbing opportunities. Try to get as many Rox as you can! In Speedy Feats, you're racing by yourself, so you don't have to worry about going super fast. (At least for now...you will be racing with other Moshlings in the Ulti-Moshling Contest races!)

The Rox in the game have the same values as in the Wooly Wilderness: a blue gem = 1 Rox, green = 3 Rox, pink = 5 Rox, and purple = 10 Rox. You can really rack up the Rox by playing Speedy Feats!

If you bump into an object, you'll be frozen for a few seconds, and unable to move. You'll also lose one of your three hearts, so be careful not to lose them all or your race is over. Sometimes, you might want to run into an object to nab some valuable Rox, even if it slows you down (as long as you have enough hearts!).

Rapid Matches and Quik Wits

Rapid Matches and Quik Wits are games of intellect that can boost a Moshling's level or your zoo's level. There are two ways you can get to the Rapid Matches and Quik Wits mini-games:

Uh oh! Prof. Purplex is hungry, dirty, and even running low on smarts! Help him get back to his usual self by choosing a mini-game icon on the bottom of the screen.

Go to your zoo, click on a Moshling, and you'll see its status (bars show how low it is in food, cleanliness, and intellect). Click on one of the icons on the bottom of the screen to play that game and get your Moshling fed, bathed, and trained! When you play the mini-game by selecting a Moshling to train, the game automatically chooses between Rapid Matches or Quik Wits.

Raarghly's Starcade offers the same games you can find by selecting a Moshling to play, but without the option to train a certain Moshling. You can still earn lots of Rox, though.

Or, go to your zoo and enter Raarghly's Starcade. Inside, you'll find Quik Wits and Rapid Matches rooms. Enter either room to play games and earn Rox! You'll get some spending money, but you won't be able to select and train a Moshling if you play this way. Your zoo level will get a boost, though.

Rapid Matches and Quik Wits are very similar mini-games; they are both timed challenges with words, colors, numbers, and matching. You earn 10 Rox for each correct answer, and a bonus of 100 more Rox if you've set a record, so you can earn a total of up to 250 Rox per game!

In Rapid Matches challenges, you drag the correct answers in place; the game won't let you drag the wrong answers into place, so you get more than one chance at the right answers for each question (until the time runs out for that question). In Quik Wits challenges, you click on the right answer from multiple choice options, but this game will let you choose the wrong answer, so you only get one try per question.
Choose carefully!

Look at all the Rox you can rack up!

Rapid Matches

Alphabetter

Place the letters in the slots in alphabetic order.

Dot Dilemma

Move the colored dots so that no matching colors are connected.

Mathemixics

Place the pieces to complete the math problem.

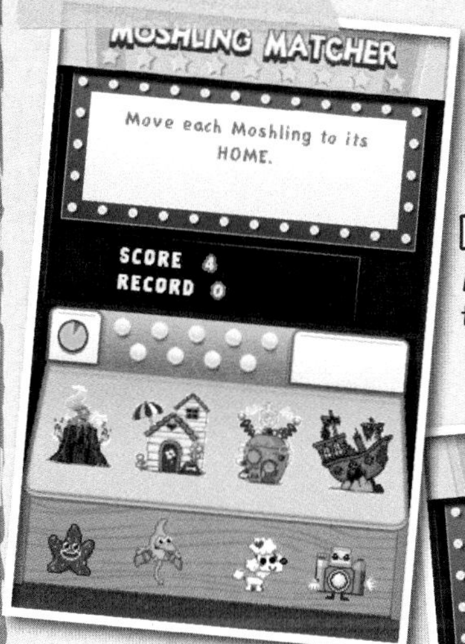

MOSHLING MATCHER

Move each Moshling to its HOME.

SCORE 4
RECORD 0

Moshling Matcher

Move each Moshling to its home.

PESKY POLYGONS

Move each shape to its MATCHING SLOT.

SCORE 6
RECORD 0

Pesky Polygons

Move each shape to its matching slot.

PUZZLING PIECES

Move each puzzle piece to its MATCHING SLOT.

SCORE 10
RECORD 0

Puzzling Pieces

Move each puzzle piece to its matching slot.

Total Test

Place the numbers so that each group adds up to 10.

TOTAL TEST

Place the numbers so that each group ADDS UP TO 10.

SCORE 7
RECORD 0

| 5 | 1 | 0 | 0 | 6 | 0 | | 4 |
| 1 | | 6 | | 2 | | 0 | 0 |

4   6   3   2

Quik Wits

COLOR COUNTER

Add up all of the RED NUMBERS.

SCORE 14
RECORD 15

3	2	1	4	5	7	3	9
8	6	0	7	6	1	7	2
5	1	3	9	8	2	5	6
9	7	8	2	5	6	7	9

19   40   25   33

Color Counter

Add up all of the red numbers.

COUNT AMOUNT

Which shape is made of the MOST SQUARES?

SCORE 9
RECORD 14

Count Amount

Which shape is made of the most / least squares?

MASTERING THE MINI-GAMES

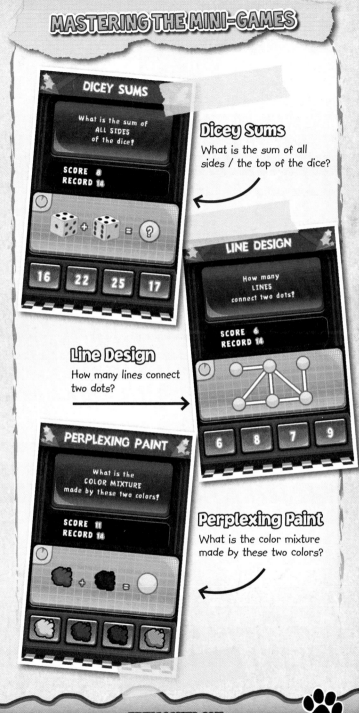

Dicey Sums
What is the sum of all sides / the top of the dice?

Line Design
How many lines connect two dots?

Perplexing Paint
What is the color mixture made by these two colors?

SECRET SEQUENCE

Which number comes next in the
NUMBER SEQUENCE?

SCORE 3
RECORD 14

25, 28, 31, _ ?

33   34   26   29

Secret Sequence

Which number comes next in the number sequence?

SHIMMY SHAPES

How many
TRIANGLES
do you see?

SCORE 8
RECORD 0

1   2   3   4

Shimmy Shapes

How many rectangles / triangles / squares do you see? Here's a tip: If you're asked to count the rectangles, count the squares, too. But if you're asked just to count the squares, don't include the rectangles in your count.

Ulti-Moshling Contest

This is it: the competition you and your Moshlings have been training for! Make sure your chosen Moshling is leveled up and extra strong in intellect and racing games, especially. Try to play the Ulti-Moshling Contest with each Moshling in your zoo! You'll get a trophy, and it's good to bond with your Moshlings.

Welcome to the competition!

You're racing the other Moshlings, but they won't collect Rox while they race. The Rox are just for you!

The contest host, Max Volume, tells you about the upcoming events: Speedy Feats, Battle of Brains, and Competition of Cuisine. These are the same mini-games you've been playing, so you and your Moshling are well prepared to take a shiny trophy back to the zoo.

There is a difference between the Ulti-Moshling Contest games versus the mini-games: in the contest games, you're also racing the other (automatically chosen) Moshlings in your event! The judging factors in how fast your Moshling completed the event.

The race is on!

After each event, the judges will give you a score based on your speed and accuracy.

The Ulti-Moshling Contest version of Speedy Feats features longer versions of familiar races and obstacles, but this time, your goal is to hit the fewest obstacles and be first to the finish line! Sometimes you might want to run into an obstacle to get ahead: since your Moshling "blinks" and can't hit any object for a few seconds after hitting another one, you can bypass tricky obstacles in that time, going straight through them.

Ring in with your answer as fast as you can, Blurp! Don't worry if your competitors ring in before you. They might be wrong. Stanley here chose the wrong answer.

The Battle of Brains score not only includes how many correct answers you give, but also how quickly you answer. (And those other Moshlings seem awfully speedy!) Ol' Buster here might not be the fastest around anymore, but my Moshlings sure are quick! If you've got to choose between being fast or being right, choose being right. Take your time if you need to, and play the games well. Even if you think the other Moshlings have beaten you because they got their answers in first, they might not be the right answers.

In the Competition of Cuisine, you must make and serve the correct meals as quickly as you can. You're competing with the other Moshlings, but this is the only game where you don't actually see your competitors. Do your best to serve up the grub as quick as you can, and you'll find out how you did compared to the others after the game is over.

The overall winner of the Ulti-Moshling Contest is based on all three events' scores. (Even if your Moshling could use a little more training, you'll at least take home a third-place trophy!) You can visit your trophies in the zoo's Visitors' Center and admire all of your Moshlings' hard work.

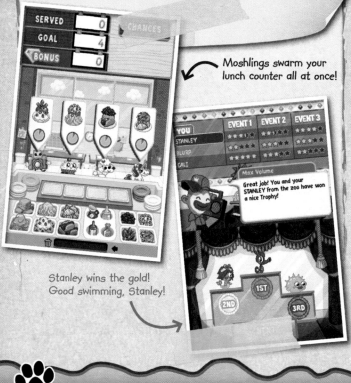

Moshlings swarm your lunch counter all at once!

Stanley wins the gold! Good swimming, Stanley!

Congratulations, Moshling collector! You've reached the heights of every Moshling hunter's dreams: a full zoo, packed with beautiful habitats and boo-tiful Moshlings. Train and play with them all, and see if you can get gold trophies for each one! But most of all, have fun watching your Moshlings and their babies in your zoo. There's nothing better than that for a truly expert Moshling collector like me...and you!

Happy hunting,
Buster

PRIMA OFFICIAL GAME GUIDE

Written by Kate Abbott

The Prima Games logo is a registered trademark of Random House, Inc., registered in the United States and other countries. Primagames.com is a registered trademark of Random House, Inc., registered in the United States. Prima Games is an imprint of Random House, Inc.

Product Manager: Jesse Anderson

Design & Layout: Melissa Smith
                  Jamie Bryson

Manufacturing: Stephanie Sanchez

Prima Games would like to thank: Gina Clarke, Mary Casey, Andy Matjaszek, Jack McCall and the rest of the Moshling Zoo team.

Important:

Kate Abbott worked at Prima Games as an editor for 5 years, and is delighted to have gotten to write this Prima guide. She's currently getting her MFA in creative writing at UC Riverside–Palm Desert. She's completed a YA novel set in Disneyland and has been a contributing editor for a Disney parks-focused newsletter. Kate's favorite Moshlings are Tiki, Prof. Purplex, and DJ Quack. She likes birds.

Kate wants to sincerely thank the great group of people at Prima Games for being so much fun to work with over the years. For this project, special thanks to Andy Rolleri and Shaida Boroumand, Jesse "Manly Enough to Handle a Sky Pony" Anderson, Jamie "Cupcake on Wheels" Bryson, and Melissa "Psycho Gingergirl" Smith. And thank you to Brad Abbott and our toddler Henry, for always understanding that when Mommy said she had to work, she meant she was going to play a video game.

ISBN 978-0-307-89216-4

Printed in the United States of America

11 12 13 14 LL 10 9 8 7 6 5 4 3 2

Prima Games

An Imprint of Random House, Inc.

3000 Lava Ridge Court, Suite 100

Roseville, CA 95661

www.primagames.com